OLBRICH BOTANICAL GARDENS

Olbrich Botanical Gardens is owned and operated by the City of Madison Parks Division with support from the Olbrich Botanical Society.

*N*o greater mistake can be made than the belief that taste and aesthetic sense is a monopoly of the merely well-to-do or purely a product of formal schooling. The park proposed is intended primarily to bring back into the life of the worker confronted by the dismal industrial tangle, whose forces we all so little comprehend, something of the grace and beauty that nature intended us all to share. For this park has not a passive, but an active function. It is not to stand aloof, a treasure of the city, beautiful, still, reserved. This park above all others, with a warmth and strength of love—of love of all the working world—should hold out its arms, should invite them to itself, until its naturalness and beauty enter into their lives.

—Michael B. Olbrich, 1921
From a speech proposing a garden site
on Starkweather Creek near Lake Monona

OLBRICH BOTANICAL GARDENS

Growing more beautiful

SHARON CYBART & JERRY MINNICH, EDITORS

Prairie Oak
PRESS

A division of Trails Media Group   *Black Earth, Wisconsin, USA*

Published for Olbrich Botanical Society by Prairie Oak Press, a division of
Trails Media Group
P. O. Box 317
1131 Mills Street
Black Earth, Wisconsin 53515

Designed and produced by Flying Fish Graphics, Blue Mounds, Wisconsin.
Printed in Korea
Front cover photo: Sharon Cybart
Back cover photo: Jeff Epping

A portion of the proceeds from the sale of this book will benefit Olbrich Botanical Gardens.

Library of Congress Cataloging-in-Publication Data

Olbrich Botanical Gardens : growing more beautiful / edited by Sharon
Cybart & Jerry Minnich.
      p. cm.
  ISBN 1-879483-85-8 (hard cover) — ISBN 1-879483-86-6 (soft cover)
  1. Olbrich Botanical Gardens (Madison, Wis.) 2. Olbrich Botanical
Gardens (Madison, Wis.)—Pictorial works. I. Cybart, Sharon. II.
Minnich, Jerry.
  QK73.U62 O426 2002
  580′.7′377583—dc21
                                        2002000184

INTRODUCTION

The old Garver Feed Supply was originally the "sugar beet factory."

$\mathcal{I}$n the mid-1920s, I first saw the area which is pictured on the pages that follow. I was in the company of my parents. The view was dominated by what was then described as the "sugar beet factory."

My father envisioned the area as a potentially attractive refuge for those local residents whose lives, otherwise, might be blighted by the dreariness of their surroundings. I think he was attempting to persuade Mother that his notion was not totally quixotic. Mother, like many others, saw only an ugly piece of real estate.

Well, Mother was wrong—the ugliness to which she objected has since been transformed into a place of great beauty; Dad was wrong as well—the appeal of the area now reaches way beyond the "locals;" my twin brother and I were wrong, too—the "sugar beet factory" did not turn out to be the place of mystery and enchantment that five year olds could imagine it to be.

What has transpired since the early days has been outlined elsewhere. I find that history to be exciting and inspiring. What stands out particularly to me is the dedication of the persons, past and present, who have been charged directly with the care and nurture of this treasure. In addition, one must be impressed by the fact that a host of people, in the area and beyond, individually and as members of organizations, has volunteered time, energy, and yes, financial support in order to further advance the development of the property.

For the contributions of all these persons, we should all be very grateful.

—Michael Emil Olbrich
March 21, 2001

The fundamental importance of plants for the planet cannot be overestimated. The Olbrich Botanical Gardens in Madison, Wisconsin, with its huge collection of living plants, teaches about the diversity of the Plant Kingdom and the importance of plants in our lives economically, culturally, and aesthetically.

The garden, with its well-interpreted collections of plants, illustrates the crucial importance of plants to the environment, the major threats that face the world's flora, and the consequences of plant extinction.

Olbrich Botanical Gardens not only provides an important community resource at the local level but also an excellent model for botanic gardens regionally, nationally, and indeed internationally.

—Peter Wyse Jackson, Secretary General
Botanic Gardens Conservation International

Bloodtwig dogwood, *Cornus sanguinea* 'Winter Beauty'

OLBRICH . . . *Madison's Public Garden*

An oasis of beauty overlooking the shores of lovely Lake Monona, Olbrich Botanical Gardens is the jewel in the crown of the Madison park system. Olbrich Botanical Gardens serves as the center of a remarkable urban greenspace, connected by bike paths and waterways to a dazzling array of recreational facilities, including a swimming beach, baseball diamonds, and a sledding hill.

Fourteen acres of spectacular display gardens draw visitors from around the world to experience Olbrich's uniquely Midwestern interpretation of the fine art of garden design. From the lush, waving grasses in the Perennial Garden to the brave spring bulbs in the Meadow Garden, Olbrich celebrates the horizontal lines and almost inconceivable hardiness of the Wisconsin landscape, inspiring and educating homeowners, students, and plant lovers of all ages. The bustling Olbrich Botanical Center, with its prairie-style design, welcomes an endless, enthusiastic stream of plant sales, gardening classes, receptions, and meetings. The soaring glass pyramid of the tropical Bolz Conservatory offers people of all ages an affordable escape from Wisconsin's harsh winter winds as it nurtures the lives of hundreds of exotic and endangered rainforest plants.

A haven for schoolchildren and scientists, family gatherings and gardeners, walkers and wedding couples, Olbrich Botanical Gardens is proud to serve both as museum and community center, treasured by the people of Madison and admired by hundreds of thousands of visitors each year. In this increasingly complex world, Olbrich offers us all a place to pause and relax, a place to find peace in the beauty of the plant world and comfort in the promise that spring will always come again.

—Dawn Bedore Proctor
Olbrich Botanical Society

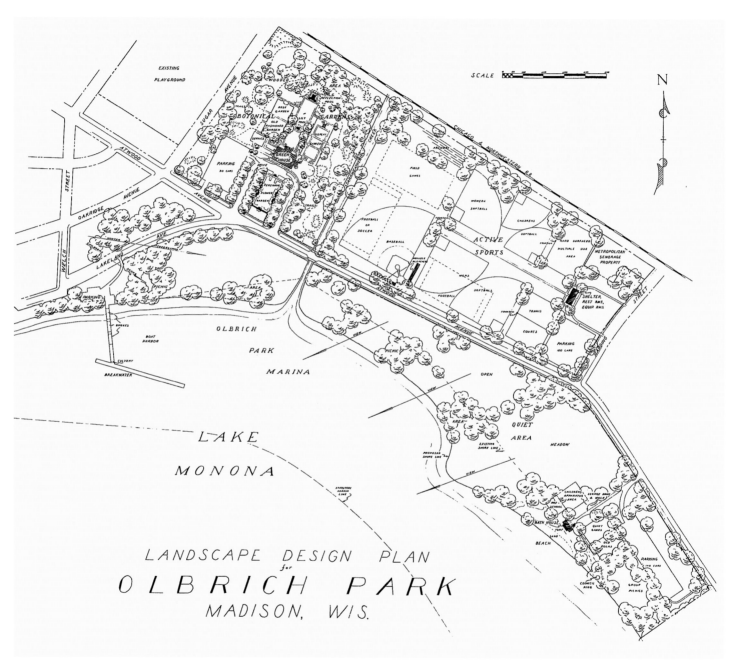

Michael Olbrich's vision for a park, 1925.

OLBRICH BOTANICAL GARDENS *History*

The beautiful gardens and conservatory buildings that now comprise the Olbrich Botanical Gardens are the result of the collective work of thousands of people who have labored unstintingly for more than fifty years to make them a reality. But neither the gardens nor the larger park that surrounds them would exist today if it had not been for the vision, the energy, and the generosity of just one man, Madison attorney Michael B. Olbrich.

Michael Balthazar Olbrich was born in 1881 on a farm in McHenry County, Illinois. In 1898 he entered the University of Wisconsin and his outstanding success there, particularly as a debater, soon brought him to the attention of another former farm boy and celebrated University debater, Wisconsin's famous reform governor, Robert M. La Follette. Meeting La Follette made a deep impression on Olbrich and fused his interest in the law with a lasting interest in politics, and it also provided him with a mentor whose cause he would champion throughout his life.

After graduating from the University Law School in 1905, Olbrich began his own law practice in Madison. Professional success came quickly and Olbrich's active campaigning on behalf of La Follette soon made him an influential figure in state Republican Party circles as well.

Olbrich was also deeply influenced by the example of another Madison attorney, John M. Olin, the longtime president of the nationally known Madison Park and Pleasure Drive Association, a private organization that had created Madison's outstanding park system. In Olin, Olbrich found both inspiration and a perfect model for living a life that united a career in the law with a passion for social betterment and a love of the natural world. Olin was deeply committed to the belief that exposure to the beauty of the natural world was essential to general well-being and he believed that a constantly expanding system of public parks was the best way to bring this beauty into the life of the average city dweller. Ill health forced him into retirement in 1911, but his work in creating parks and in preserving the beauty of Madison's natural setting inspired a new generation of civic leaders, of whom Michael Olbrich was to prove the most important.

Olbrich was especially interested in the preservation of direct public access to Madison's lakeshores and to Lake Monona in particular. This emphasis on Lake Monona arose out of Olbrich's concern that the residential areas on Madison's east side that were being developed adjacent to the factories along Williamson

Street and Atwood Avenue were lacking in adequate park facilities. Olbrich saw that new residential developments were moving inexorably towards the lakeshore and he realized that only prompt action would save the still vacant shoreline at the east end of Lake Monona.

In 1916, Olbrich's attention focused on what was then a badly polluted marshland that bordered both sides of Starkweather Creek at the east end of Lake Monona. In its place he envisioned a sweeping expanse of park curving along the lakeshore, a park whose crowning feature would be a municipal flower garden set in its midst. This park would then be linked to a parkway that would follow the north shore of the lake all the way to the recently completed parkway that bordered both sides of the Yahara River.

Michael B. Olbrich

Single-handedly, Olbrich set about acquiring this property, using his own money and concentrating first on the area bordering Starkweather Creek. His first purchase gave him control of almost 2,700 feet of shoreline, which he then offered to the city at cost providing that the new park was named "La Follette Park." This condition proved unacceptable to many due to La Follette's opposition to World War I so Olbrich kept the land, adding 800 more feet to the total in the next three years and bringing his personal commitment to almost $40,000. In 1919, after La Follette requested that his name not be used, Olbrich repeated his previous offer to the city. This time support for Olbrich's proposal was widespread. Olin and the Park and Pleasure Drive Association brought in noted Chicago landscape architect Ossian C. Simonds to draw up a development plan for the new park. Olbrich then led two successful community-wide fund-raising drives to secure additional parcels of land and on July 22, 1921, the city took title to its newest park.

In 1922 Olbrich formed the Madison Parks Foundation to raise the money necessary to complete the new park and to acquire the shoreline between it and the Yahara River parkway. By 1928, both goals had been achieved and Olbrich then turned the attention of the Foundation to the acquisition of the first portions of the University of Wisconsin Arboretum on the shore of Lake Wingra. When Olbrich died unexpectedly in 1929, the city council responded by naming the new park at the east end of Lake Monona Olbrich Park in his honor and in recognition of the remarkable legacy he had left to his adopted city.

Without a doubt, the new park had required something of a visionary to see its potential when Olbrich first began to assemble it in 1916. The character of the site, its size, and even its shape were much different from what we see today. In that day the shoreline of Lake Monona came to within one hundred feet of Atwood Avenue opposite today's Botanical Gardens and most of the land within the park boundaries was an unusable and unappreciated marsh that was seriously polluted by the effluents discharged by the adjacent United States Sugar Company's beet processing factory.

During Olbrich's lifetime, the only part of the park that was truly usable was the playground area that is still located just to the west of today's Botanical Gardens. The remaining land awaited implementation of O.C. Simond's 1920 development plan, but no action was taken on this major project until 1931, when the city took over the parks system created by Olin and his Association and promoted James G. Marshall to be the head of the new Parks Department.

Marshall's first task was to coordinate the large work crews that were being organized by the city's Outdoor Relief Committee and the effect of these crews on Olbrich Park was immediate. Atwood Avenue's path through the park was straightened and the old roadway was torn up. The debris then became part of the fill that the city deposited in its newly designated municipal dumping ground, located in the marshy area east of Starkweather Creek between Atwood Avenue and the railroad tracks. Marshall then screened this area with trees and set his crews to work improving the existing playground area and the stretch of land along the lakeshore. By 1933, these projects, mostly completed, were complemented by the tree and flower planting activities of neighborhood organizations like the East Side Business Men's Association and the Madison Garden Club.

By late 1935, enough work had been done on the park to make the comprehensive planning of its future both feasible and necessary. Consequently, Marshall oversaw the preparation of the first master plan for the development of the park. This plan was especially notable for including the first preliminary plan for what would eventually become today's Botanical Gardens. The proposed gardens, though quite different in design from what was actually built, were intended from the first to be located where the gardens are today. Unfortunately, this 11.5 acre site was still largely a peat bog and marshland in 1935, and its development lay far in the future.

The ensuing years saw the gradual filling in of all the marshy areas within the park's boundaries. The east end of Lake Monona and Starkweather Creek were both dredged and the sandy fill that resulted was then used to extend the shoreline of the park further out into the lake and to fill in low-lying areas such as the gardens site.

Construction of the first part of the gardens, February 1953.

By 1950, the process of turning marshland into parkland was largely complete and most of Olbrich's dream of providing the east side with recreation space and lake access was a reality. All that remained was to crown this work with the flower gardens that Olbrich had hoped might one day grace the site.

The first work towards establishing the Gardens began in 1952 when the Olin Trust Fund gave the Madison Parks Commission $22,688 to begin development. This resulted in the construction of twin shelter buildings and in the large formal space behind them that was originally the Rose Mall. Another grant from the Olin Fund in 1957 gave the Gardens its first greenhouse, a structure that was soon expanded to serve as an informal center for area gardeners.

By the early 1960s, however, it was understood that a real garden center building was necessary in order to fully realize the garden's potential. This led to the formation in 1962 of the Garden Center Club, a volunteer group whose members were to work ceaselessly over the next decade to establish such a center. In the meantime, the Gardens continued to grow in size and in beauty. More greenhouses were erected and in 1965 the Olin Fund made possible the construction of the John M. Olin Fountain. By 1971, the success of the steadily growing Garden Center Club and its fund-raising efforts enabled it to commission Madison architect Stuart Gallaher to design a new Garden Center building. A major fund-raising effort finally made this elegant building a reality and it was dedicated in 1978 at a cost of $380,000.

The creation of the new Garden Center, now called the Atrium, was accompanied by the establishment of the Olbrich Botanical Society in 1979, a membership organization whose 6,629 current members now handle the garden's fund-raising and educational activities. The Society promptly redoubled efforts to expand the Gardens themselves. This resulted in the new Rose Garden, Perennial Garden, Herb Garden, All-America Garden, and the Alpine Rock Garden. In 1986, more than 60,000 persons visited the gardens, which also hosted 345 special events.

The success of the expanded Gardens, however, created a demand that the existing Garden Center was unable to fulfill. As a result, in 1986, Stuart Gallaher was again commissioned to design a greatly enlarged Botanical Center adjacent to his earlier Garden Center building. The Society then took up the challenge of raising the $4,600,000 needed to build it. Spearheaded by the Bolz family's offer to fund construction of the Botanical Center's diamond-domed conservatory in honor of Adolph C. and Eugenie Mayer Bolz, the campaign ultimately raised more than three-fourths of the total amount from private sources, including more than 2,500 individuals, 80 area corporations and 15 private foundations.

The completion of the new Olbrich Botanical Center complex, in 1991, was a milestone event in the history of Madison. The magnificent new Bolz Conservatory and its stunning tropical plant collection not only dramatically increased the numbers of people coming to the Gardens but it also turned the Gardens into a year-round attraction. Almost equally important but less visible was the construction in 1992 of two new production greenhouses, which gave the Gardens staff 10,000 square feet of energy-efficient growing space. Together, these two wonderful facilities ushered in a new era for the Gardens and set the stage for future development.

Now that it possessed facilities that a much larger city might envy, the Gardens staff began to focus attention on the outdoor gardens. Nineteen ninety-two saw the first phase of the Wildflower Garden begun and the construction of the Arlette Morse Terrace, which welcomes visitors who enter the Gardens from the Botanical Center. Even more important, though, was the development of a new strategic plan for the entire Gardens.

That a new plan was needed had become obvious by this time. In 1993 alone, more than 167,000 people toured the Gardens, 100,000 more than in 1986, putting considerable stress on the existing outdoor gardens and on the circulation system of paths that linked them. In addition, new specialty gardens were needed, existing ones like the popular Perennial Garden needed to be expanded, and others, such as the All-America Garden, needed to be phased out in order to make room for gardens that were better suited to new needs.

In 1993, a new Olbrich Gardens Master Plan, developed jointly by Ken Saiki Design of Madison and Sasaki and Assoc. of Massachusetts, was completed, becoming the blueprint for the development of the Gardens for the rest of the decade. In order to implement the first phase of the plan, the Society embarked on a million dollar capital campaign in 1994 to fund the construction of the Gateway Rose Arbor, the restoration of the old Sunken Garden, and construction of a new Perennial Garden. So great was the support for this campaign that fully 85% of the total was pledged by the end of the year, with the rest coming in the following year. Another legacy of the campaign was the founding of the Olbrich Circle and the Olbrich Stewardship Fund, an endowment fund for the maintenance of the Gardens.

Construction on these projects began in 1995, along with other improvement projects funded by the City of Madison Parks Division. By the end of the year a new footbridge designed by architect Paul Graven linked the Wildflower Garden to the Rock Garden, work had begun on the renovation of the Sunken Garden, a Children's Garden had been established, and the first phase of the new Gateway Rose Arbor was in place.

And yet, even with all these projects being pushed forward, the ever increasing popularity of the Gardens was a source of concern as well as pride. In 1996, for example, 216,000 people visited the fourteen-acre Gardens, more than three times the number who had visited in 1986. Providentially, though, an opportunity arose in 1996 to purchase five additional acres of land adjacent to the Gardens that was owned by the Garver Feed Co. which occupied the former beet processing factory. At the same time, the City of Madison decided to transfer two additional contiguous seventeen plus-acre parcels that it owned to the Madison Parks Department for use as parkland and for Gardens expansion. Together, these two adjacent parcels totaled 23 acres and it was immediately realized that they could, if consolidated, almost triple the size of the existing Gardens and give the Society control of all the land north of the Gardens between S. Fair Oaks Avenue and Starkweather Creek.

Because the expansion possibilities offered by acquiring both of these parcels were so extraordinary, the Society immediately launched a $750,000 campaign in 1997 to purchase the Garver property. Thanks to a major gift from the American Family Insurance Co. and large gifts from several other sources, this goal was met later in the year. Suddenly, the future expansion of the Gardens was assured. As a result, the Society and the Gardens staff found themselves faced with a range of possible options that had been the stuff of dreams only the year before. Fortunately, the process that had resulted in the 1993 Master Plan for the Gardens

The Rose Mall in its infancy, c. 1955, now the Sunken Garden.

provided a proven model for a way in which to take advantage of this unprecedented opportunity. Once again, the Botanical Society Board and members of the Gardens staff created a strategic plan to guide those who would develop a new Master Plan for the Gardens. With this plan in place the same team of Ken Saiki Design of Madison and Sasaki and Assoc. of Massachusetts that had developed the 1993 Master Plan set about creating a new master plan aided by Bowen Williamson Zimmerman, Inc., of Madison, a creative process that would not be completed for another two years.

In the meantime, previously planned expansions of the existing Gardens continued. Even while the new land was being acquired, large gifts from the John A. Johnson Foundation and the Eugenie Mayer Bolz Family Foundation, in 1997, brought the restoration of the Sunken Garden and the construction of the new

Donor's Arbor to completion as well. Work also continued on completing the James Law Flowering Grove, the 1.5-acre Perennial Garden, and the Meadow Garden, and by the end of the millennial year 2000, the existing gardens were attracting national recognition.

The acceptance of the new Olbrich Gardens Master Plan late in 2000 heralds a new era for the Gardens, one that will be marked by new opportunities both planned and unplanned. Among the latter was the unexpected but welcome gift of an authentic Thai Pavilion, a gift to Wisconsin from the Thai government and the Thai Chapter of the Wisconsin Alumni Association. This beautiful open wood structure has been placed in a garden of its own just across Starkweather Creek from the existing Gardens and will be linked to it by a graceful serpentine bridge. Also now in the making is the new and greatly expanded Rose Garden, a spectacular two-acre development showcasing the hardiest roses that can be grown in Wisconsin.

Thus, Olbrich Botanical Gardens and its dedicated staff have now entered both a new century and a new millennium and, as Madison prepares to celebrate the 50th anniversary of the Gardens in 2002, new generations of supporters and volunteers will now have the opportunity to share and carry forward Michael Olbrich's enduring legacy to Madison.

—*Timothy F. Heggland*
Preservation Consultant,
Fall, 2001

The Thai Pavilion, newly completed in October, 2001,
before construction of the Thai Garden.

Spring

Daffodil, *Narcissus* 'Carlton', and Siberian squill, *Scilla siberica*, against a backdrop of Lake Monona.

*H*orticulture *Magazine* has been collaborating with Olbrich Botanical Gardens for years bringing symposia programs to its discerning audiences. Every time I visit Olbrich I know I'll be surrounded by excellence in horticulture and enquiring minds. With a magical lakeside setting, innovative designs, and great plants, what more could a gardener ask? I'm confident Olbrich's next fifty years can only be more exciting.

—*Nan Blake Sinton, Director of Programs,*
Horticulture *magazine*

The early-blooming Glory of the Snow, *Chionodoxa luciliae*, is a welcome sight as winter turns to spring.

Redbud trees, *Cercis canadensis*, and Virginia bluebells, *Mertensia virginica*, in the Wildflower Garden.

*T*hanks for the wonderful gardens you bring to our community. Through the volunteer efforts and generosity of many, all residents have access to a place of beauty, serenity, and inspiration. Olbrich Gardens have long been an important part of our thriving community. Whether serving as an outstanding venue for special events, or just as a place to stop and contemplate for a few quiet moments, the gardens are a treasure for all to enjoy.

—*Kathleen Falk, Dane County Executive*

The Wildflower Garden features the ephemeral yellow lady's slipper, *Cypripedium calceolus (above)*, and bloodroot, *Sanguinaria canadensis (left)*.

A river of daffodils, *Narcissus*—'Mt. Hood', 'Las Vegas', and 'Carlton' varieties—flows through the Atwood Grove.

The unique pyramid shape of the tropical Bolz Conservatory symbolizes Olbrich Botanical Gardens.

The Olbrich Botanical Gardens are a place of inspiration to many. There is a feeling of lively spirit here thanks to the dedicated team who strive to make this place a centre of horticultural excellence.

—*Fergus Garrett, Head Gardener*
Great Dixter, England

An ocean of tulips is a glorious spring sight.

Happy gardeners at Olbrich's annual spring plant sale.

Tulips and ornamental crabapples wrap the Lussier Terrace in spring color.

A garden is many things to many people. A sanctuary. A laboratory. A place of mystery, inspiration, frustration, admiration, elation. The Olbrich Botanical Gardens are all of these. Who has not visited these gardens without making mental notes to improve one's own garden next season? Who has not admired the sheer beauty of these gardens, so carefully tended as to conceal the effort that creates them? A garden is a bridge between our artificial world and that of nature. Here, among these gardens, we may perhaps sense that we are part of that natural world, and that with thought and practice—possibly may learn to live in grace within it.

—*Jerry Minnich*
author of The Wisconsin Garden Guide

Common bleeding heart,
Dicentra spectabilis

For the nine hundred-plus members of our state organization, the Wisconsin Garden Club Federation, meeting in Madison at Olbrich shares the warmth of "going home" with the fellowship of gardening friends and informed companions.

One could say that Olbrich Botanical Gardens is "a force for good." In today's world of stress and tension, the relaxed education of gardening is much needed in our society.

—*Jule Schoenike, Past President*
Wisconsin Garden Club Federation

(left) A young volunteer plants a rose bush.

(opposite) Olbrich's annual indoor Spring Flower Fest offers the hope of spring while snow is still on the ground outside.

Cold-tolerant lettuces combine to make a colorful early spring container garden.

(above) The Meadow Garden, studded with jewel-toned spring blooms, offers a no-mow alternative to the standard high-maintenance lawn.

(left) Slimleaf tulip, *Tulipa linifolia*

The Rock Garden is at its peak of color in spring.

*I*t is the atmosphere of learning that I value most about Olbrich, on every level, from the world-class horticultural seminars, through the elementary children's programs, and directly from the gardens themselves. This is no accident, but a conscious effort of management and staff. I find it impossible to make even the most casual visit without learning something wonderful.

—Joan Severa
author of *Creating a Perennial Garden in the Midwest*

Ballustrades from Madison's Olin Terrace add historical character to Olbrich's indoor Spring Flower Fest.

This stylized Thai garden scene, featured in Olbrich's Spring Flower Fest, was inspired by the new Thai Garden.

The Spring Flower Fest features an artistic interpretation of the new season.

*B*eing a part of Olbrich as a contributor and volunteer makes your day as you associate with some of the finest people in our town.

—*John C. Weston*
John A. Johnson Family Foundation

Summer

$\mathcal{W}$e are extremely pleased to be a part of the Olbrich Gardens experience. This is a place where the wonders and beauty of nature are on display for our community to enjoy, and a place where we can teach the importance of a sustainable healthy environment. The visions of Olbrich's founders fifty years ago, and of Olbrich's contemporary benefactors, have produced this jewel in our city.

—John Bolz
Bolz Family Foundation

The Sunken Garden features unique combinations of plants in cool colors.

Golden hops, *Humulus lupulus* 'Aureus', rambles about the mixed border of butter yellow yarrow, *Achillea* 'Moonshine', and silvery foliaged wormwood, *Artemisia ludoviciana* 'Valerie Finnis'.

A sculpture by Rose Van Vranken is reflected in the Sunken Garden pool.

Long shadows create a restful atmosphere in the formal Sunken Garden.

(right) Ornamental onion, *Allium aflatunense* 'Purple Sensation'

"Fiddlehead" fern sculpture by Sylvia Beckman.

*I*t was a joy to watch this bulky man tenderly nurse a rose into loveliness. But the care he lavished on a rose garden was a symbol of something deeper. Whether he was tending a rose or throwing his boundless energy into the development of parks . . . the dream that drove him on was the dream of the beautiful life for himself and his fellows.

—*University of Wisconsin President Glenn Frank, October, 1929, Speaking about Michael B. Olbrich, community leader and founder, Olbrich Botanical Gardens*

(above) Climbing rose, *Rosa* 'Fourth of July'

(opposite) 'The Hunter' shrub rose
Insets: Hybrid tea roses
top: 'Secret'
bottom left: 'Double Delight'
bottom right: 'Chicago Peace'

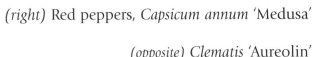

(right) Red peppers, *Capsicum annum* 'Medusa'

(opposite) Clematis 'Aureolin'

A traditional prairie flower, Kansas gayfeather, *Liatris pycnostachya*.

*W*hether leading a tour of students, professionals, avid gardeners, or just looking for ideas for my own garden—I find Olbrich a valuable resource, packed full of good ideas. I always leave with new things to borrow or share.

—Melinda Myers
Milwaukee Area Technical College Instructor
Author, The Garden Book for Wisconsin
and Month by Month Gardening
in Wisconsin

Container gardens liven up every patio corner.

The purity of a snow white late panicle hydrangea, *Hydrangea paniculata* 'Unique'.

The formal courtyard garden is one of several specialty gardens in the Herb Garden.

These boys are proud of the lettuce they raised themselves
in Olbrich's Children's Garden.

*O*lbrich Gardens is a product of its people, the community, and about reaching for possibilities. It is possible to achieve unique, high quality, planning, design and implementation with a small local consulting firm. It is possible to continue to raise money for construction, operations, and maintenance in a community the size of Madison, and finally, it is possible to partner with the City of Madison and the University of Wisconsin to bring Olbrich's Thai Pavilion and Garden here, the only one of its kind in North America. It is the vision of the Gardens' staff and the Olbrich Botanical Society Board to accomplish great things now and still preserve the possibilities for future generations to do the same.

*—Ken Saiki, Landscape Architect
and President of
Ken Saiki Design, Inc.
Master planning and design of
garden expansion*

Summer annuals bloom in drifts of color.

The sunflower, *Helianthus* 'Lemon Queen', in the Rock Garden radiates a soft glow on a summer afternoon.

*O*lbrich Botanical Gardens is a leader in educating the public on the crucial relationship between flowering plants and their pollinators. They are teaching people about the environment and our fragile world in the best way possible—with beautiful display gardens, classes, and outreach programs. I have every confidence that such a thoughtful and perceptive organization will continue to be on the cutting edge in horticulture and education.

—Angela Overy, Founder, Denver Botanic Gardens School of Botanical Illustration and author of Sex in Your Garden

An eastern tiger swallowtail butterfly, *Papilio glaucus*, sips nectar from a butterfly bush, *Buddleja davidii*.

An eclectic combination of bright colors and textures brings vibrancy to the Perennial Garden.

Fall

Autumn crocus, *Colchicum* 'Lilac Wonder'

Showy stonecrop, *Sedum spectabile* 'Brilliant'

Fall color frames the Olbrich pond.

The bright yellow sunflower, *Helianthus decapetalus* 'Capenoch Star', stands out against the ornamental grass, *Miscanthus sinensis* 'Grosse Fontane', in the Perennial Garden.

"Spring," a sculpture by Sylvia Beckman, echoes the form of newly emerging leaves.
The sculpture was a gift from William and Joyce Wartmann.

Unique carnivorous plants, *Sarracenia alabamensis x psittacina* and *Penthorum sedoides*,
grow in a hand-made bog trough.

*M*adison boasts dozens of distinctive attractions for visitors, including the lovely and sublime Olbrich Gardens. The Gardens' physical beauty, award winning exhibits, and programming treats are must-see's and do's on thousands of visitors' itineraries. And, with the unveiling of Olbrich's Thai Pavilion and Garden, the leaders of our City and Olbrich Gardens once again prove that this institution is one of our destination's greatest treasures.

—Deborah T. Archer
President, Greater Madison Convention
& Visitors Bureau

The delicate white flowers of *Gaura lindheimeri* 'Whirling Butterflies' imitate their namesakes.

Cardinal flowers, *Lobelia cardinalis*, lend bright red accents to the ornamental grass, *Miscanthus sinensis* 'Helga Reich', in the Perennial Garden.

(above) Japanese kerria, *Kerria japonica* 'Golden Guinea', backed by ornamental grass, *Miscanthus sinensis* 'Grosse Fontane', in the Perennial Garden. *(right)* Indian grass, *Sorghastrum nutans* 'Sioux Blue'

(opposite) The Sunken Garden explodes with color.

The prairie-style architecture of the Donor's Arbor is framed by a fluffy ring of fall-blooming ornamental grasses, *Miscanthus sinensis* 'Adagio' and 'Nippon'.

(right) Common witchhazel, *Hamamelis virginiana*

The Herb Garden features many specialty gardens including the kitchen garden,
dye garden, medicinal garden, and formal knot garden.

Aquatic plants add color, form, and texture to the Perennial Garden ponds.

The annual quilt show at Olbrich Gardens is a grand event for me because gardening and quilting go together. Gardening is like quilting the earth—patches of beautiful colors, designs, textures, borders, paths reminding me of the sashing in a quilt. Just looking at gardens or quilts gives me warmth.

—Mary Spaay, President of Mound Vue Garden Club,
Olbrich Botanical Society member,
and Garden visitor for 30 years

The Reflecting Pool in the Sunken Garden provides a visual connection to Lake Monona beyond.

Winter

ears were shed in the 1960s when Josephine Brasci and her grapevine were uprooted from Madison's old Greenbush neighborhood. Shade and grapes of the vine had been a source of culture and pride for the Sicilian-born woman and her family since it was planted in 1920. Today, the Brasci grapevine continues to grow in Olbrich Gardens casting patterns of sunlight and shade over engraved bricks as a reminder of Madison's historic settling of Italian immigrants.

—*Catherine Tripalin Murray, author of the historical Italian cookbooks* A Taste of Memories from the Old "Bush" *and* Grandmothers of Greenbush

The grapevine, *Vitis sp.,* twines around the entry arbor in the Herb Garden.

Frost softens the leaves of lantanaphyllum viburnum,
Viburnum x rhytidophylloides 'Willowwood'.

Lingering fruit stems on an ornamental crabapple sparkle with frost.

Snow highlights the symmetry of the Herb Garden Arbor.

*I*nch for inch, this relatively small conservatory rivals any in the country in terms of community devotion. Maybe it is because the place is a warm, fragrant oasis in the long Wisconsin winter, but annual attendance has more than tripled at Olbrich Botanical Gardens since the conservatory was built.

—*Crystal Palaces: Garden Conservatories of the United States*

Dried blossoms of late panicle hydrangea, *Hydrangea paniculata* 'Tardiva', glow against a wintery backdrop.

A snowy Lussier bridge connects the Rock Garden and Wildflower Garden.

Snow outlines the design of the prairie-style Donor's Arbor.

Olbrich's Holiday Express provides entertainment for all with model trains and a festive poinsettia forest.

Bolz Conservatory

The Bolz Conservatory is the largest microcosm of the tropics in the Madison area, and I take my Tropical Plant Diversity class there each fall. It's a learning resource and a year-round oasis, with special exhibits and lush tropical plants bordering the paths. At the canopy level, the trees are constantly threatening to burst through the glass, so Conservatory Curator John Wirth and his staff periodically go in and trim back, much as a wind storm or a tree fall in the tropics would temporarily open up a gap in the forest cover.

—*Paul E. Berry, Botany Professor and Herbarium Director*
University of Wisconsin-Madison

Bridge over the koi pond.

Gardenia, *Gardenia jasminoides*

he Gardens provide a wonderful respite on cold winter days. They are a window onto another world that is fecund, tropical, diverse, beautiful, and comforting. A wonderful addition to Madison life.

—*William S. (Bil) Alverson*
Environmental & Conservation Programs
The Field Museum, Chicago

The Orchid Aerie offers changing displays of Olbrich's extensive orchid collection.

(above) Monarch, *Danaus plexippus,* and Queen, *Danaus gilippus,* butterflies sip nectar from buddleja.

(right) Parrot flower, *Heliconia sp.*

(above) The Conservatory's carnivorous plant collection includes this unique pitcher plant, *Sarracenia sp.*

(opposite) Vanda orchid, *Vanda coerulea*

Creating a beautiful garden contributes to the quality of life for the whole community.

—*Nancy Ragland*
Director, Olbrich Botanical Gardens

(*above*) White peacock butterfly, *Anartia jatrophae*

(*left*) Two hundred and twenty misting nozzles provide humidity for the plants and give the Conservatory a realistic rainforest haze.

THE STORY OF THE FIRST BUILDING—THE *Atrium*

Irene Straus, lifetime member of the Olbrich Botanical Society and long-time Olbrich neighbor:
"In the 1970s the Olbrich Garden Club, formerly the "Garden Center Club," kept on having plant sales to raise money for the first building at the Gardens, which would be called the Atrium . . . "

Former Madison Mayor Paul Soglin:
" . . . Eight to ten women came to see me. They were raising $15 to $20 a weekend by selling plants. It was very clear that at the rate things were going, despite their hard work, nothing was going to be built in their lifetimes, or my lifetime, or their grandchildren's lifetimes . . . "

Irene Straus:
" . . . Mr. Soglin was Mayor at that time, and was very favorable. I was asked to make a presentation to the Madison City Council telling of the many uses for such a building . . . ."

Paul Soglin:
" . . . These women were so convincing we decided, 'Let's put it in the budget' . . . I can say in all honesty that if these ten women had not asked for an appointment with me and quietly explained why they needed the facility, it never would have happened."

The Atrium was designed by Madison architect Stuart Gallaher, and dedicated in 1978.

Volunteers work on the annual beds in front of the Atrium.

I started volunteering because I wanted to give something back. I've enjoyed Olbrich so much over the years. Now, it's fun. I love talking with the visitors.

—*Elisabeth Kunske, Garden Greeter*

THE STORY OF OLBRICH'S *Thai Pavilion & Garden*

*O*lbrich's Thai Pavilion is a rare treasure and a work of art. The fourth to be built outside of Thailand, Olbrich's pavilion is the only one in the continental United States, and the only one surrounded by a lush Thai-style garden. The pavilion was a gift from the Thai government and the Thai Chapter of the Wisconsin Alumni Association to the University of Wisconsin-Madison. The UW-Madison gave the pavilion to the City of Madison, which owns and operates Olbrich Gardens. Olbrich's beautiful public gardens provide an ideal setting for this cultural treasure.

The pavilion was assembled on-site by skilled artisans from Thailand using traditional Thai construction techniques. No nails, screws, or metal fasteners of any kind were used. The pavilion bears the Royal Seal of the Thai Crown, gold leaf etchings, and a lacquer finish. In Thailand, pavilions are sited near water and are most often used for celebrations or to escape the rain and heat of the day.

Olbrich's unique Thai Garden emphasizes texture and form. Carefully chosen winter-hardy plants create a serene tropical garden in the heart of the Midwest. The garden includes glazed water jars and Thai clipped tree art known as *mai dat*. Only the sacred lotus plant, revered in Thailand, grows in the reflecting pools. An ornamental bridge leads from Olbrich's Serenity Garden to the Thai Pavilion, linking the gardens and symbolically bridging cultures.

The Thai Pavilion was assembled at Olbrich in the fall of 2001.

ศาลาไทย ประกอบขึ้นที่โอลบริคในฤดูใบไม้ร่วง ปี ๒๐๐๑

เรื่องของศาลาไทย และ สวนโอลบริค

ศาลาไทยแห่งโอลบริค เป็นงานศิลปกรรมอันล้ำค่า เป็นศาลาไทยเพียงแห่งที่สี่ ที่สร้างนอก
ประเทศไทย และเป็นศาลาไทยเพียงแห่งเดียวในทวีปอเมริกาเหนือ และเป็นแห่งเดียวที่แวดล้อม
ด้วยสวนไทย

ศาลาไทยเป็นอภินันทนาการจากรัฐบาลไทย ร่วมกับสมาคมศิษย์เก่าของมหาวิทยาลัย
วิสคอนสิน-แมดิสันมอบให้ และมหาวิทยาลัยวิสคอนสิน-แมดิสันมอบศาลานี้ต่อให้แด่เมือง
แมดิสัน ซึ่งเป็นเจ้าของและผู้จัดการสวนโอลบริค สวนสาธารณะอันสวยงามแห่งนี้ เป็นสถานที่
ในอุดมคติสำหรับสมบัติแห่งวัฒนธรรมอันล้ำค่านี้

ศาลาไทยได้รับการประกอบเข้าเป็นรูปร่างในสถานที่แห่งนี้ ด้วยกลุ่มช่างผู้เชี่ยวชาญ
จากประเทศไทย โดยใช้วิธีการก่อสร้างแบบไทยโบราณ ไม่มีการใช้ตะปู หรือสลักเกลียว
หรือตัวยึดที่เป็นโลหะใดๆ ในการประกอบส่วนต่างๆ เข้าด้วยกัน ศาลาไทยได้ประดับ
พระปรมาภิไธยย่อ แห่งพระบาทสมเด็จพระเจ้าอยู่หัวรัชกาลที่ ๙ ประดับมงกุฎ และลงรักปิดทอง
ในประเทศไทย ศาลาไทยจะต้องอยู่ใกล้น้ำ และมักจะใช้เป็นสถานที่สำหรับการเฉลิมฉลอง
หรือเป็นที่หลบฝนและแสงแดด

เอกลักษณ์สวนไทยแห่งโอลบริค เน้นที่รูปแบบ ลักษณะและขนาดของต้นไม้ ต้นไม้ที่ทนต่อสภาพ
ฤดูหนาวได้ถูกคัดเลือกอย่างละเอียดถี่ถ้วน ปลูกให้เป็นสวนต้นไม้เมืองร้อน ที่สงบร่มรื่นในใจกลาง
แห่งภาคตะวันตกกลาง สวนประกอบด้วยอ่างน้ำเคลือบและไม้ดัด บัวซึ่งเป็นดอกไม้สำคัญ
ในประเทศไทยจะปลูกไว้ในสระน้ำเท่านั้น สะพานจากสวนเซเรนิตี้แห่งโอลบริค นำไปสู่ศาลาไทย
เพื่อเชื่อมโยงสวนทั้งสอง และเป็นสัญลักษณ์แห่งการเชื่อมวัฒนธรรมทั้งสองเข้าด้วยกัน

—Thai translation by Sidhorn Sangdhanoo and Robert J. Bickner,
Department of Languages and Cultures of Asia, University of Wisconsin-Madison

Community members were invited to sign the back of individual tiles,
which were then attached to the roof by Thai artisans.

ชุมชนได้รับเชิญไปลงนามในแผ่นกระเบื้องที่ปูหลังคาศาลาไทย โดยช่างไทย

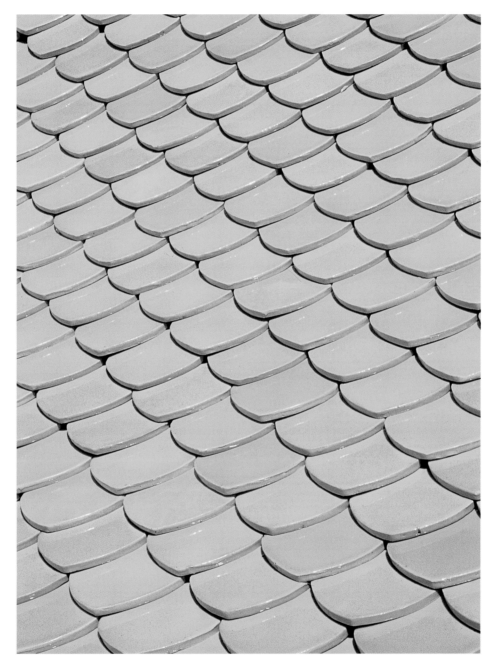

Detail of roof tiles gleaming in the sun.

รายละเอียดของกระเบื้องหลังคาที่ส่งประกายในแสงอาทิตย์

ABOUT THE PHOTOGRAPHERS

SHARON CYBART has worked as Public Relations Coordinator for Olbrich Botanical Gardens since 1991. She has directed Olbrich's promotional efforts for more than a decade, during which annual attendance at the Gardens has more than tripled. Sharon's photographs have been an integral part of that effort, appearing in many local, regional, and national publications. Her photos of the Bolz Conservatory are featured in the book *Crystal Palaces: Garden Conservatories of the United States.* Sharon edits the *Olbrich Garden News,* a quarterly publication of the Olbrich Botanical Society. Before joining the Gardens, she was a radio journalist, a freelance writer, and a freelance photographer. She is an avid gardener in her spare time.

JEFF EPPING joined the staff as Director of Horticulture at Olbrich Botanical Gardens in 1994. He oversees the design, planting, and maintenance of more than 14 acres of display gardens. Jeff's planting designs in the Perennial and Sunken Gardens have won several awards and he is currently working on innovative designs for the new tropical-style Thai Garden and prairie-style Rose Garden. Jeff's photography reflects his keen interest in ornamental plants and garden design for beauty in every season. His garden images, taken throughout the Midwest and England, have appeared in many local and regional journals and gardening books.

CHRISTIAN HARPER has been a Horticulturist at Olbrich Botanical Gardens since 1992. He is curator of the Rose Garden which, in 1997, won the annual Presidents Award from All-America Rose Selections as the best public display garden in the United States. Christian is also curator of the Rock and Wildflower Gardens and oversees the design and planting of the Gardens' extensive spring bulb displays. Christian photographs both for enjoyment and to document the plant collections. His background in art can be seen in his sense of color and design, both in Olbrich's Gardens and in his photographs.

(opposite) The Royal Seal of the Thai Crown graces the Pavilion entrance.

ตราพระปรมาภิไธยย่อ ประดับมงกุฎ ประดับอย่างงดงามเหนือทางเข้าศาลาไทย

PHOTO CREDITS